What Did Jesus Do?

Stories about
Honesty & Forgiveness

MARY MANZ SIMON
ILLUSTRATED BY ANNE KENNEDY

Tommy
NELSON

Thomas Nelson, Inc.

Nashville

For Matthew Michael Simon, 3 John 4
—Mary Manz Simon

For Mom, a "big soul,"
from Annie, a "little soul"

Text copyright © 1998 by Mary Manz Simon
Illustrations copyright © 1998 by Anne Kennedy

Published in Nashville, Tennessee, by Tommy Nelson™, a division of Thomas Nelson, Inc.
Managing Editor: Laura Minchew; Editor: Tama Fortner

Scripture quotations are from The Holy Bible, New Century Version, copyright © 1987, 1988, 1991 by Word Publishing, Nashville, Tennessee. Used by permission.

Library of Congress Cataloging-in-Publication Data

Simon, Mary Manz, 1948–
     What did Jesus do? : Stories about honesty and forgiveness / Mary Manz Simon ; illustrated by Anne Kennedy.
          p.   cm.
     Summary: Relates two stories dealing with contemporary problems, then presents flashbacks to Biblical times to see what Jesus did in similar situations.
     ISBN 0-8499-5857-1
     1. Honesty—Juvenile literature. 2. Forgiveness—Religious aspects—Christianity—Juvenile literature. 3. Bible stories, English—N.T. Gospels. 4. Jesus Christ—Example—Juvenile literature. [1. Honesty. 2. Forgiveness—Religious aspects—Christianity. 3. Bible stories—N.T. 4. Christian life.] I. Kennedy, Anne, 1955– ill. II. Title.
     BV4647.T7S47   1998
     241'.4—DC21   98-7247
                                                                                              CIP
                                                                                               AC

Printed in the United States of America
98 99 00 01 02 03 WCV 9 8 7 6 5 4 3 2 1

To the Adult

As an educator and mother of three, I care deeply about helping children develop a set of core values.

Many adults and older children embrace the "What would Jesus do?" concept. But developmentally, because young children cannot mentally change places with someone else, they can't think how someone else would respond in a specific instance. As a result, the WWJD phenomenon has had minimal impact on younger children.

However, young children copy and personally internalize behaviors modeled for them. That's why the book you hold in your hands illustrates what Jesus actually did in situations similar to those that children face every day. By looking at what Jesus did, even young children can learn to look to Him for answers to problems today.

Dr. Mary Manz Simon

Honest to Goodness

A Story about Honesty

"Whew! I'm hot," Cole said, draining the last few drops from his water bottle.

"With that tournament coming up, Coach is really making us run," Kate said.

"Aw, you're just not in shape," said Jason, as he sauntered by. "I played so well, I'm going to treat myself to some ice cream." Jason nodded toward the frozen delights painted on the delivery truck parked in front of the convenience mart.

Kate, Cole, and Amanda
watched their teammate
stroll toward the store.

"Just looking at that ice cream cools me off," Cole admitted.

"You *must* be hot, if even a picture looks good," Kate said
with a chuckle.

Jason watched his teammates out of the corner of his eye. But
he was *more* interested in the boxes being unloaded off the truck.

The driver jumped into the back of the truck and scratched his head. "Hey, kid," he called down. "You see another box?"

Jason shrugged.

The driver glanced around, then rolled down the back door and jumped to the ground.

"Short a box," he mumbled to himself as he climbed into the cab and slammed the door.

"Hey, guys," Jason called to his teammates. "Look what I found."

Steam rose as he pulled the box out into the sun.

"A breathing box," Amanda giggled.

"The truck driver must have forgotten it," said Cole, glancing suspiciously at Jason.

Jason looked over his shoulder. They were alone in the lot. "Help yourself," he offered.

"That would be stealing," Cole said. "We can't do that. Remember the story in church last week? The one where Jesus talked about honesty."

"I love being rich," Zacchaeus said with a satisfied, if somewhat evil, smile. He was a tax collector, and charging people more taxes than they really owed had made him a wealthy man.

This day began like any other day. But something happened that changed not just the way Zacchaeus collected taxes, but his whole life.

Jesus came to town.

Wherever Jesus went, huge crowds gathered, as he healed and taught the people. On this day, Jesus was walking through the city of Jericho when a crowd began to gather near the tax table.

Now Zacchaeus was curious about Jesus. He wanted to see who was pulling people away from his tax table. But there were so many people lining the streets, he couldn't see Jesus.

Zacchaeus tried to stand on a rock, but he slipped off.
Zacchaeus tried to climb on a camel, but the camel would
not stay still. Then, Zacchaeus saw his answer: a tree. A
tree wasn't slippery, and a tree wouldn't move. He
scooted up the trunk and eased out on a branch. Now,
he could see Jesus.

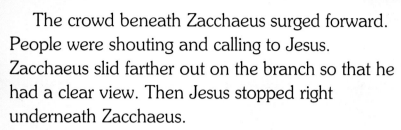

The crowd beneath Zacchaeus surged forward.
People were shouting and calling to Jesus.
Zacchaeus slid farther out on the branch so that he
had a clear view. Then Jesus stopped right
underneath Zacchaeus.

"Come down, Zacchaeus," Jesus said. "I am
going to stay at your house today."

Zacchaeus scurried down to welcome Jesus.

The people in the crowd mumbled and complained. Everyone knew about Zacchaeus. They knew he was dishonest. They knew he cheated them. They knew Zacchaeus was a sinner. The murmur in the crowd grew louder.

Then Zacchaeus told Jesus, "I will give half of my money to the poor. And I will pay back four times the amount I have cheated people. Beginning right now, I will be an honest man."

Steam still rose from the box.

"Let's get the box inside before everything melts," Cole said.

"Seems like a waste to me," Jason remarked. "Who'd miss a little ice cream?"

"But it's the right thing to do," Cole insisted. Jason shrugged as his teammates carried the box inside.

Moments later, the trio emerged from the store, smiling broadly.

"The lady at the register gave us these for free," Cole explained. "She didn't even know a box was missing."

"Being honest sure tastes good,"
said Amanda.

An honest witness tells the truth.
—*Proverbs 12:17* NCV

The Race

A Story about Forgiveness

"Your new bike is beautiful, Cole," said Amanda. She had always wanted a bike like Cole's.

"Ready to race?" asked Jason.

"Amanda and I can't race against Cole's new bike," said Kate.

"Aw, come on," said Jason.

Kate shrugged her shoulders. With a reluctant "Okay," she and Amanda pedaled to the usual starting line. Jason gave the countdown, and the trio whizzed off. Right at the start, Cole zoomed ahead.

"You were right," Amanda called to Kate. "We can't win against Cole anymore!"

As they reached the finish line, Amanda skidded in a cloud of gravel and dust. Her tire hit a rock, and she careened into Cole's bike. Tumbling onto the gravel path, Amanda and both bikes fell in a jumbled heap.

"Are you all right?" Kate asked cautiously.

"I think so," Amanda said slowly. Turning around, she saw Cole kneeling by his new bike. The front wheel cover had smashed into the tire.

"Oh, Cole, I'm so sorry!" said Amanda.

"That's okay," he said softly. "At least you weren't hurt."

The group looked silently at the bent metal.

"I'll help you carry the bike home so the tire won't get cut," Jason offered.

"Thanks," Cole said, then added, "Amanda, I'm really glad you didn't get hurt."

"Thanks," Amanda said.

Later, at Kate's house, Amanda waited for her dad to pick her up.

"I'm really sorry I messed up Cole's bike," Amanda said.

"But he forgave you," Kate reminded her. "'Forgive' means 'forget,' remember?"

Amanda smiled, remembering the last time she had heard the word, 'forgive.'

Jesus told this story about a man with two sons.

"Dad," the younger son said to his father. "I don't want to stay here and work. I want my share of the family's money now. I want to have fun."

Soon the boy left home with his treasure.

He threw big parties. He spent money everywhere. He wore rich clothes. He ate fabulous meals. He made friends with famous people.

He had a terrific time until he ran out of money. Then, his new friends left. He sold everything, but he still didn't have enough money to live.

His clothes wore out. His sandals fell apart. And his stomach growled all the time. He finally got a job feeding pigs.

"Here piggy, piggy," he called. He was so hungry, even the pig's food looked good!

As the well-fed pigs rolled in the mud, the young man thought back to his wonderful life at home. He remembered his father and the servants and the good food.

"I will return home," he decided. "I will ask my father to forgive me. I will beg him to hire me as a servant."

As he started home, he thought again and again about asking for forgiveness. Would his father forgive him? Or, would he send him away as he deserved?

When the father saw his son stumbling down the road, he ran out to meet the boy.

The son knelt in the dusty road and said hoarsely, "Father, I have done terrible things. I wasted all the money." The son sobbed. "I made many mistakes. Father, I am so very sorry."

Tears stained the boy's dirty face. His father's heart softened as he accepted his son's apology.

"Everyone, be glad with me!" the father shouted to his servants. "Let's celebrate. My son has come home!"

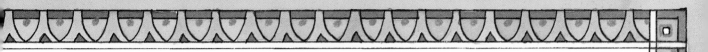

"Bring him new sandals, new clothes, and an expensive ring. Set a great feast," the father continued.

The son was amazed as people rushed around to serve him. He felt so blessed. He had made terrible mistakes, but his father had forgiven him.

Toot, toot.

Headlights shone through the window. Amanda hurried
outside to the familiar car.

"Sorry I'm late, honey," said her dad, reaching to lift her bike
into the trunk. "I didn't expect the meeting to last that long."

"No problem," Amanda said tiredly.

"So you forgive me?" her dad asked, reaching to give her a hug.

"Forgive you?" Amanda asked, looking up with surprise.

"Yes, forgive me for being so late," her dad repeated.

"Of course, Dad," Amanda answered with a smile. "I know how good it feels to be forgiven."

Forgive, and you will be forgiven.
—*Luke 6:37 NCV*